I Am Not A Grasshopper

Claudia Matozzo

WestBow Press books may be ordered through booksellers or by contacting:

WestBow Press
A Division of Thomas Nelson & Zondervan
1663 Liberty Drive
Bloomington, IN 47403
www.westbowpress.com
844-714-3454

ISBN: 978-1-6642-9835-4 (sc)
978-1-6642-9836-1 (e)

Library of Congress Control Number: 2023907576

Print information available on the last page.

WestBow Press rev. date: 06/26/2023

I Am Not A Grasshopper

God's people, the Israelites, were slaves in Egypt for hundreds of years. They were forced to work extremely hard and were treated with cruelty. They cried out to God to save them, and God sent Moses to help rescue them. With God's direction, Moses led the people to the land that God had promised to give them many years earlier to their ancestors. On the way to the Promised Land, God showed His people many miracles. He opened the Red Sea so they could cross on dry land to safety, He sent manna from Heaven every day for them to eat and He even led the way through the desert so they would know the way they should go. He led them at night with a pillar of fire and during the day by a pillar of smoke. God took loving care of His people.

After many months of traveling, the Israelites reached a place very close to the Promised Land. God told Moses to send 12 men to spy out the land. Moses told the spies to report back to him everything they could about the land. He wanted to know what the land looked like and what kind of people lived there. He also asked them to bring back some of the fruit that was growing in the land.

The spies spent 40 days exploring the land. They walked through the mountains, and they walked through the valleys. They saw the people that lived there and discovered that some of them were giants! They picked different kinds of fruit to bring back too. They discovered the grapes that grew there were so big that two people had to carry one cluster of grapes!!

When the spies returned, they gave Moses and the rest of the people a report of the things they had seen in the land. The 12 spies agreed that the land was beautiful and able to grow and produce delicious fruit and other foods to eat. The 12 spies agreed that the cities were built strong and the people that lived there were strong too. They also agreed that there were giants who lived in the land.

Two of the spies were named Caleb and Joshua. With great confidence they said, "Let's go and take the land! We can do it!" The other ten spies did not agree with Caleb and Joshua. They said, "No! We can't do it. The people in the land are too big and too strong for us. They'll destroy us! When we were there, we felt like grasshoppers and we seemed like grasshoppers to them too."

The ten spies felt like small grasshoppers that could be easily stepped on or destroyed because they had forgotten all the wonderful miracles God had done for them as they traveled. They had forgotten that they were God's special people and that He loved them very much. They forgot that with God on their side they would be victorious over their enemies.

The Israelites became very scared and upset because of all that the ten spies were saying. They were so upset that they began complaining. They even said they wanted to go back to Egypt and be slaves again! Joshua, Caleb, and Moses tried to calm them down. Joshua told them not to be afraid because God was with them, and God would help them. But they refused to listen. They believed the other 10 spies.

The people were afraid and felt like grasshoppers too. They forgot God was their faithful rescuer and provider. Sadly, because they complained and did not trust God, they were punished. God said they were not allowed to ever enter the land. Instead, they had to wander around and live in the desert for 40 years. God said their grown children and their families would be allowed in, but not them.

17

Joshua and Caleb knew they were not grasshoppers because they remembered that God is great and mighty. Since their wonderful and mighty God was always with them, they could be strong and courageous people in any situation. God wants you to know that you are NOT a grasshopper. He wants you to remember who He is so that you will know who you are.

Sometimes, people we meet might make us feel like a small, powerless, unimportant grasshopper. When that happens, God wants you to remember these Bible promises....

God is your Creator. That means you are a masterpiece.
Thank you for making me so wonderfully complex! Your workmanship is marvelous—how well I know it. Psalm 139:14

God is your Heavenly Father. That means you are loved.
See how very much our Father loves us, for He calls us His children, and that is what we are! 1 John 3:1a

God fights for you. That means you are victorious.
For the Lord your God is going with you! He will fight for you against your enemies, and He will give you victory! Deuteronomy 20:4

God is your Savior. That means you can be saved.
"For this is how God loved the world: He gave his one and only Son, so that everyone who believes in Him will not perish but have eternal life. John 3:16

God is your provider. That means you are taken care of.
And this same God who takes care of me will supply all your needs from His glorious riches, which have been given to us in Christ Jesus. Philippians 4:19

God gives you strength.
That means you can do all things through Christ.
For I can do everything through Christ, who gives me strength. Philippians 4:1

Loved

Victorious

Masterpiece

Strong

Saved

Printed in the United States
by Baker & Taylor Publisher Services